Foundations in Trinitarian Thought and Theology

Foundations in Trinitarian Thought and Theology

*

A Biblical Explanation of the Doctrine of the Trinity

Written by: Roderick L. Evans

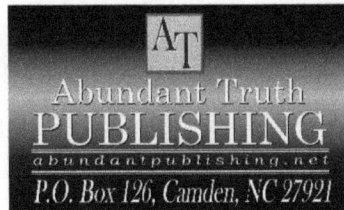

AT

Abundant Truth
PUBLISHING
abundantpublishing.net
P.O. Box 126, Camden, NC 27921

Foundations in Trinitarian Thought and Theology
A Biblical Explanation of the Doctrine of the Trinity

Front & Back Cover Designs by Abundant Truth Publishing

Abundant Truth Publishing
an imprint of Abundant Truth International Ministries

For information address:
Abundant Truth International
P.O. Box 126
Camden, NC 27921

Unless otherwise indicated, all of the scripture quotations are taken from the *Authorized King James Version* **of the Bible. Scripture quotations marked with NIV are taken from the** *New International Version* **of the Bible. Scripture quotations marked with ASV are taken from the** *American Standard Version* **of the Bible. Scripture quotations marked with GW are taken from the** *God's Word Bible.*

ISBN 13: 978-1-60141-300-0

Printed in the United States of America.

Contents

Chapter 1:

The Fullness of the Divine Nature

Colossians 2:9

Great is the mystery of God! Paul, in his writings, shows us that the life, ministry, death, and resurrection of Jesus Christ clarify the mystery of God.

> And without controversy great is the mystery of godliness; He who was manifested in the flesh, Justified in the spirit, Seen of angels, Preached among the nations, Believed on in the world, Received up in glory. 1 Tim 3:16 (ASV)

Christ came to provide salvation to the world and reveal the true and living God. Christ came as an obedient Son to make known the Father's counsel, wisdom, and might.

> And this is life eternal, that they might know thee the only true God, and Jesus Christ, whom thou hast sent. John 17:3 (KJV)

Jesus expressed in His prayer to the Father the purpose of His coming – to make known unto men the only true God, which is the Father, and that they would know Christ, whose coming was from the Father; intending to free men from the bondage of sin. Both Testaments agree that all things are done by the will of the Father. Biblical accounts reveal the character and nature of God.

With these things in view, let us look more closely at godhead. Some scholars and ministers try to explain Godhead by implying that it refers to God being revealed as Father, Son, and Holy Ghost; that is, the Trinity. However, godhead has nothing to do with the makeup of God, or His work in Jesus Christ by the Holy Ghost. It simply refers to His divine nature.

In the King James Version of the Bible, the term godhead is used three times by Paul. In these instances where we find the word godhead, each is derived from three Greek variations (theiotēs, theios, and theotēs) of the same word - theos. This term simply means divinity or godlike. Godhead refers specifically to the nature of God or that which characterizes who He is.

In understanding the meaning of godhead and examining how Paul used this term, we can develop a solid understanding of the Godhead.

The Divine Nature is Distinctive

Extensive travelling and evangelizing characterized Paul's ministry. After preaching the gospel in Berea, Paul went to Athens. While waiting for others to come, he was stirred in his spirit because of the rampant idolatry. He saw an altar built to the unknown god. He used this as a catalyst to present the only true and living God. It was in this discourse that he used the term godhead.

> Forasmuch then as we are the offspring of God, we ought not to think that the Godhead is like unto gold, or silver, or stone, graven by art and man's device. Acts 17:29 (KJV)

Paul introduces the Athenians to the distinctiveness or the uniqueness of the godhead. Athenians worshipped gods that were made by man's hands. They were inanimate and existed through man's devices or imaginations.

He, conversely, stated that all men were the offspring of God (in support of God's creation of the first man). Men were living creatures, having a will, thoughts, emotions, feelings, and volition, which is a clear reflection of the Godhead (divine nature). This was in stark contrast to the gods and idols they worshiped.

He told the Athenians not to think that God's nature could be reduced to objects, altars, buildings, ignorant worship, and rituals. This statement reveals the fallacy of the statement that one can find God in everything and in all things. Paul told them: do not misunderstand the nature of God, thinking He can be reached through man-made forms of religious worship, devotion, and service. He told them that God, in His divine nature, is commanding all men to repent and come to Him in order to escape His judgment.

> And the times of this ignorance God winked at; but now commandeth all men everywhere to repent. Acts 17:30-31 (KJV)

His divine nature demanded that He be approached through a personal relationship, which is now available through repentance and faith in His Son. The Godhead is unique in that God gives one way for men to approach Him unlike other deities and beliefs that say that there are other ways to know God and serve Him and enter into eternal life.

The Divine Nature is Incontrovertible

Paul, in his letter to the Romans, outlined the foundational truths of the Christian faith. He related how men, in the beginning, knew God but transformed their knowledge of the true God into lies and remade Him in the likeness of man, animals, and the hosts of heaven.

He also stated that the wrath of God is revealed from heaven upon men who suppress the truth in unrighteousness. He revealed that God had manifested Himself to all men and showed Himself to all men. This is possible because all men are the offspring of God (Acts 17:29). It is within this context that we can understand Paul's second use of the term godhead.

> For the invisible things of him from the creation of the world are clearly seen, being understood by the things that are made, even his eternal power and Godhead; so that they are without excuse. Romans 1:20 (KJV)

From this, we discover that the Godhead (nature of God) is incontrovertible or undeniable. Men can know and understand who God is and what He wants. This is what aids men in their reception of the gospel of God revealed in Jesus Christ.

Oftentimes, men feign ignorance in order to avoid submission to the righteousness of God. Satan, who blinds the eyes of people so that they will not receive the truth, further solidifies this. Despite these dynamics, Paul states that all men can understand God's eternal power and divine nature (Godhead) because it is clearly seen in creation.

He then gives us a history lesson by recalling the early inhabitants of the earth. He stated that they knew God and what He wanted but suppressed that knowledge and created the various forms of worship. Though many forms of false worship exist today, knowing and receiving the truth of God is attainable because of how man was created.

Remember, God breathed into Adam's nostrils. He imparted a portion of Himself in the first man who was to procreate. It is that same breath of life that permeates through men today. Therefore, Paul said men are without excuse in not coming to God because there is an inner witness of God in all, by virtue of creation.

The Divine Nature is Cohesive

Paul's final use of the term godhead is in his letter to the Colossians. He wrote to the Colossians to bring them back to the gospel of God revealed in Christ. Erroneous teachings had come to them to make them depend on other supernatural beings and religious ordinances rather than on the work of Christ.

In his defense of the complete work of God in Jesus Christ, Paul stated that everything they wanted to know about God was manifested in the life, work, and ministry of Christ.

For in him dwelleth all the fullness of the Godhead bodily. Col 2:9 (KJV)

Paul states that the fullness of the godhead; that is, the fullness of the nature of God was in Christ while He walked on the earth. Therefore, the

Colossians did not have to trust in any other practice, doctrine, or thought, but only upon Christ because God completed the work of salvation through and by Him.

One must understand that it is through the divine nature that the Father, Son, and the Holy Ghost are cohesive or unified. They each share the same nature, though they are distinct in personhood. Again, this is how they are one and yet separate because the same nature and divinity (godhead) characterized the being of them all.

Many confuse the unity of the Father and Son with the Father and Son being one and the same. However, throughout the scriptures, we find the Father and Son are distinct (which will be fully discussed and substantiated in this book) yet possessing the same nature.

In understanding these dynamics of the

godhead, we can understand the mystery of God, which is revealed in Christ. When we understand that Christ came to introduce men to the Father in word and deed, we will understand the greatest mystery of God, revealing Himself in Christ.

Chapter 2:

And God Said

Genesis 1:26

Christians know, by faith, that God created the heavens, the earth, and the universe. The biblical record states it in this manner,

> In the beginning God created the heaven and the earth. And the earth was without form, and void; and darkness was upon the face of the deep. And the Spirit of God moved upon the face of the waters. Gen 1:1-2 (KJV)

In the first two verses of Genesis, we discover that God is not alone. The Holy Spirit's presence is noted alongside God as He began His creative work. The manifestation of God's power reflected in the Holy Spirit's presence was established at the entrance of the biblical record.

The Creation of Man

As we read further in Genesis, we see that through God's spoken word that the heavens, the earth, the skies, the seas, and all manner of living creatures were created. However, the crown of God's creation (man) was not present.

As God declared His intent for the creation of man, His language and approach changed. Throughout the creative process, God held no conversations. He just declared what He wanted, and it was so. However, in this instance, we discover that throughout the creative process, someone else was present with God.

And God said, Let us make man in our image, after our likeness…Gen 1:26a (KJV)

These words have confused men for centuries and have sparked numerous discussions, arguments, and debates. Yet, we must remember that God is not trying to confuse us or leave us in ignorance when it comes to understanding Him.

Some interpret this verse to mean that God was just talking to Himself as an individual does at times. God saying "Let us" is comparable to individuals who say, "Let's see what I will do" though they are speaking to only themselves. The primary fallacy of this interpretation is that God is definitely not like man. He is perfect in thought, way, deed, and words. He will say what He means and mean what He says.

Some will say that it is still possible. Well, that is true. Nevertheless, if God said "Let us" as a personal reference, then the text would read, "Let us make man in my image and my likeness." However, it does not.

To substantiate that God meant "Let us" in the plural sense, we read that He repeats "our" twice (in OUR image, after OUR likeness). Therefore, when it states that God said, "Let us," He was speaking to another.

For those who have studied the Genesis account in the Hebrew, there are no Hebrew words for "let" and/or "let us" in the creation account. In the creation account, let and let us is not present in the original texts. The text reads something like this, "And God said, Be light," and so on. When we come to God's creation of man, it reads like this, "And God said, Make man in our likeness and after our image."

The rendering in the Hebrew dissolves any confusion as to whether God was using a colloquialism or was He speaking to/concerning someone else. Clearly, He is acknowledging the presence of another during creation. But who?

We have noted that the Holy Spirit was present with God. Could He have been speaking solely to the Spirit of God? The answer is simply "no." Though the Holy Spirit is a person, unlike God, we see Him as an invisible presence who permeates the hearts of men and accomplishes the will of God in the earth.

Even as Jesus taught the disciples concerning the Holy Spirit's coming, He said that the Holy Spirit would not speak of Himself, but would reveal Christ and only speak what He hears,

> But when the Comforter is come, whom I will send unto you from the Father, even the Spirit of truth, which proceedeth from the Father, he shall testify of me. John 15:26 (KJV)

> Howbeit when he, the Spirit of truth, is come, he will guide you into all truth: for he shall not speak of himself; but whatsoever

he shall hear, that shall he speak: and he will shew you things to come. John 16:13 (KJV)

Jesus and the Holy Spirit both proceeded from God but, in the aforementioned verses, the relationship between the Father and the Son is different from the Father's relationship with the Holy Spirit.

The Fullness of Times

In every place where the Holy Spirit is mentioned, He is always seen pointing men to God and carrying out God's plan and purposes. Though Christ did the same, He came as the express representation of God; an attribute never bestowed upon the Holy Spirit.

Who being the brightness of his glory, and the express image of his person. Heb 1:2-3 (KJV)

Who is the image of the invisible God, the firstborn of every creature. Col 1:15 (KJV)

Therefore, Christ is seen as begotten in God's image, both in form and personality. Hence, God could not have been speaking solely to the Holy Spirit because He is never said to possess the image and/or likeness of God, though He exists eternally as God.

However, the New Testament writers clearly demonstrated that what can be said of the Father can also be said of the Son. We can assuredly state that God had to speak to another who possessed His image and likeness, which could only be Jesus Christ. Some will say, "How can we be certain that God was s peaking to Christ when He is not mentioned by name?

The New Testament apostles and writers help us to understand the presence of Christ before

before and during creation. Before discussing this fully, we want to interject one fact. Remember, the plan of God in Christ was hidden throughout the ages. Though Christ was there, God had an appointed a time when He was to be revealed.

> But when the fullness of the time was come, God sent forth his Son, made of a woman, made under the law. Gal 4:4 (KJV)

And also,

> That in the dispensation of the fullness of times he might gather together in one all things in Christ, both which are in heaven, and which are on earth; even in him. Eph 1:10 (KJV)

In each of these passages, we discover that there was a time, set by God, when Christ would be revealed as the Son of God.

This was so that God could gather all people and things through and by Him. This is the chief reason that Christ, oftentimes, is not mentioned by name. There was a time appointed by the Father when Christ would be fully revealed.

Considering this truth, we can examine New Testament writings concerning the presence of Christ before and during creation to validate the claim that God, in fact, was speaking to Christ because He was present. We will begin by looking at the gospel of John.

In the beginning was the Word, and the Word was with God, and the Word was God. The same was in the beginning with God. John 1:1-2 (KJV)

One of Christ's titles is the Word. As John introduces his readers to the person, work, and ministry of Christ, he begins by addressing the divinity of Christ.

John begins by stating that in the beginning was the Word. This beginning noted here is not the same as the beginning stated in Genesis 1:1. John introduces his audience to the truth that at the beginning of beginnings Christ was present.

John does not imply that the Word was alone in the beginning (as some suggest) rather he is giving us a progression of how Christ came to walk among men in the flesh. Again, his opening statement is to recognize the eternal existence of Christ.

As John proceeds, he begins to clarify his opening phrase by stating that the Word was with God. Right here is where we discover that the Word never abided alone but it abided with God. We are informed of the eternal existence of Christ along with God the Father. John then goes on to write that the Word was God.

Herein lies a problem for readers. How can the Word be God and also abide with God? Because it seems to be an apparent contradiction, many interpret John's words to mean that Jesus and God the Father are one in the same. However, this is not what John is conveying. Jesus (the Word) was called God because the Father referred to Him as God. Consider the following passage,

> But unto the Son he saith, Thy throne, O God, is forever and ever: a sceptre of righteousness is the sceptre of thy kingdom. Heb 1:8 (KJV)

God refers to His Son as God. Therefore, Thomas' designation of Jesus as Lord and God does not negate the existence of the Father as God.

And Thomas answered and said unto him,

My Lord and my God. John 20:28 (KJV)

We can understand John's statement considering this: though Christ was with God, He can also be called God because of His relationship to the Father and because the Father called Christ 'God.'

We have established that Christ was with God from the beginning by John's gospel, as well as established a basis for why Christ can be called God. Since John states that the Word was with God, we know that during the creative process, Christ was with God also.

To clarify further his statements, John reaffirms that Christ and God are separate but together. He repeats himself and says that the Word (which was in the beginning, abiding with God, and was God) was in the beginning with God. This is so there would be no confusion that the

Son was always with the Father before He was manifested in the flesh.

John continues to speak of Christ by stating that He not only abided with God, but He actively participated in creation.

> All things were made by him; and without him was not anything made that was made. John 1:3 (KJV)

John brings to light something that is not apparent in the creation account. Christ participated in the creation of the world. He states that all things were made by Him. Again, this was not to make his readers think that God and Christ are the same. He qualified his statement by stating that nothing was created without Him. This demonstrates that He, with the involvement of another (God the Father), created all things. To reaffirm John's claim of Christ's presence at creation, Paul declares the same truth in his letter to the Colossians.

> For by him were all things created, that are in heaven, and that are in earth, visible and invisible, whether they be thrones, or dominions, or principalities, or powers: all things were created by him, and for him: And he is before all things, and by him all things consist. Col 1:16-17 (KJV)

Paul establishes the same truths as John. He states that Christ is before all. Again, this speaks of the eternal existence of Christ. He also states that all things were created by Him. Again, this would seem that Paul is saying that Christ and the Father are the same and that Christ was alone in creation. However, this is not what Paul is saying. He is simply reaffirming that Christ was there with God actively participating in the creative process.

Both John and Paul affirm that Christ existed

with God before and during Creation. He was an active participant. This is how we can establish that Christ, though not mentioned by name, was the one whom God spoke to. Yet, some will still say, "If Christ was present and active in creation, why wasn't He mentioned by Moses in the account?"

To understand how Moses records that God created the heavens and the earth, while not mentioning the presence of Christ even though the New Testament writers insist Christ was an active participant in creation, is not very hard to discover. Again, we need to look to the writings of the Bible. Paul makes a profound statement to the Corinthian church. Consider three translations of the following verse.

But to us there is but one God, the Father, of whom are all things, and we in him; and one Lord Jesus Christ, by whom are all things, and we by him. 1 Cor 8:6 (KJV)

"There is only one God, the Father. Everything came from him, and we live for him. There is only one Lord, Jesus Christ. Everything came into being through him, and we live because of him." 1 Cor 8:6 (GW)

Yet to us there is one God, the Father, of whom are all things, and we unto him; and one Lord, Jesus Christ, through whom are all things, and we through him. 1 Cor 8:6 (ASV)

Each translation conveys the same meaning, which helps us to understand some things. First, everything came into being through the Father. It was according to the Father's will and volition that all things exist.

Therefore, the creation account gives the ultimate credit of creation to God the Father. Remember also, there was a set time for the Son to be revealed.

Second, this verse informs us that Christ was present, according to the will of God, actively creating all things. Therefore, Paul states that BY Him and THROUGH Him are all things. So, we can understand that whenever God spoke in Genesis concerning what was to be created, Christ performed it. Therefore, we can conclude that when God said, "make man in our image and after our likeness," He was speaking of and to the Son who was present, actively involved in creation.

Therefore, in the beginning, God did create all things by and through Jesus Christ along with the presence of the Holy Spirit. In the beginning, we find that the Father, the Son, and the Holy Spirit coexisted without contradiction, but all was done through the will of God the Father. This helps us to understand that even though we worship Christ, it is done only because the one true God has instructed us to, because Christ is His Son and God has loved Him.

Chapter 3:

The God of Israel

Deuteronomy 6:4

God emancipated Israel from Egyptian bondage. They saw His miracles and His great works against the Egyptians. Now, they were to go into a land flowing with milk and honey. God, clearly, had chosen Israel from among the nations to be a light to the world. Before they could enter Canaan, God instructed Moses to teach Israel concerning His commandments, statutes, and judgments.

Now these are the commandments, the statutes, and the judgments, which the LORD your God commanded to teach you, that ye might do them in the land whither ye go to possess it. Deut 6:1 (KJV)

As Moses instructed the people, He introduced a religious concept that was foreign to most of the nations of that day: the concept of monotheism. Moses called Israel's attention to understand that they worshiped the true and living God.

Israel would serve only one God as opposed to the polytheistic nations that surrounded them. God's revelation of Himself progressed as He dealt with Israel as a nation. All of this culminated with the revelation of His Son who pointed Israel and the nations back to God, who is the Father.

Hear, O Israel: The LORD our God is one LORD. Deut 6:4 (KJV)

Through hindsight, we discover that Moses' statement alluded to the existence of Christ alongside God. However, this verse is not to be seen as a code for the existence of the Father, Son, and

Holy Spirit, but as Moses declaring God's supremacy above all gods and showing Him as the only true God.

Christ's existence does not negate this truth, but establishes it, because He endeavored to bring men back to God (John 17:3). Let us not consider some attributes of the Lord God, the Father.

The God of Israel is the "I Am" (Yahweh)

God used this name to reveal Himself to Moses. Many of the passages in the Old Testament that contain the word "Lord" is derived from this Hebrew name. Some have called it God's personal name.

Because Christ referred to Himself as "I Am," proponents of the Oneness doctrine say this substantiates that God and Christ are one and the same. However, this is not true. Christ was establishing His eternal presence by claiming this distinction to Himself and the authority given to Him by the Father.

Yahweh (Jehovah) means self-existent and eternal. God revealed Himself as the One who exists by His own volition without beginning or end. Unlike the gods of the nations, God was not the figment of man's imagination or the creation of man's hands.

> Ye are my witnesses, saith the LORD, and my servant whom I have chosen: that ye may know and believe me, and understand that I am he: before me there was no God formed, neither shall there be after me. Isaiah 43:10 (KJV)

As the Self-Existent God, no other god was before Him and none will be after Him. He stands alone as the God of the universe. When God appeared to Moses in the mount, He had to declare His name to him.

> And the LORD passed by before him, and proclaimed, The LORD, The LORD God, merciful and gracious, longsuffering, and abundant in goodness and truth, Keeping mercy for thousands, forgiving iniquity and transgression and sin, and that will by no means clear the guilty; visiting the iniquity of the fathers upon the children, and upon the children's children, unto the third and to the fourth generation. Ex 34:6-7 (KJV)

God declared Himself to Moses through this personal name of the Father. God is self-existent who is longsuffering and full of mercy yet will hold men responsible for their iniquities if they walk in them.

The God of Israel is the Supreme God (Elohim)

In the Hebrew scriptures, where one fi nds the word, "God," it is often derived from this term, "elohim.". The first verse of the Bible contains this term translated "God."

In the beginning, God created the heaven and the earth. Gen 1:1 (KJV)

The term, elohim, is the plural form of the word "el" which means god. "El" was used to describe any type of deity, not just the God of Israel. Elohim can be translated "gods" or magistrates; by implication also "majesties." This poses a problem for astute students of the Bible. Though the Father and Son exist separately, the use of elohim in the scriptures is not to validate Trinitarian doctrine.

There was an appointed time for Christ to be revealed. The use of elohim was not a foreshadowing of Christ with the Father. The use of this term was to establish God's supremacy and not His plurality. Else, there would be a contradiction of revelation and thought to the Hebrews.

Since *elohim* is also translated magistrates and majesties, God revealed Himself as elohim: He was above anything that could be called god. Elohim denoted His supremacy over the 'gods' created by the heathens.

The many times one reads "I am Lord God" in the Old Testament, God is revealing Himself as the Self-existent One who is above anything that is called God: This is who the Father is.

The God of Israel is the Heavenly Patriarch (Father)

One of the chief designations of God is that of father. God is revealed as eternal and supreme. In addition, He is a Father to His servants.

> Doubtless thou art our father, though Abraham be ignorant of us, and Israel acknowledge us not: thou, O Lord, art our father, our redeemer; thy name is from everlasting. Isaiah 63:16 (KJV)

This denotes His personal feelings for His creation as loving, paternal, caring, comforter, and provider. Those that come to know Him can expect His full attention and care; including, His discipline. Even Adam was called the son of God.

> Which was the son of Enos, which was the son of Seth, which was the son of Adam, hich was the son of God. Luke 3:38 (KJV)

One of God's favorite designations of Israel was that they were His children. As God, He made Himself a Father unto them.

When Israel was a child, then I loved him, and called my son out of Egypt. Hosea 11:1 (KJV)

This type of God/Father relationship would be the principle characterization of God's involvement with man. Hence, we see Jesus coming as the Son of God to bring men into a Father-child relationship with the Supreme God.

The God of Israel is the Bridegroom (Husband)

Through His dealings with the children of Israel, we discover that God also revealed Himself as husband. This denotes the intimate relationship that God forms with man.

For thy Maker is thine husband; the LORD of hosts is his name; and thy Redeemer the Holy One of Israel; The God of the whole earth shall he be called. Isaiah 54:5 (KJV)

As a husband and wife are committed to one another and become one, God enters this type of relationship with those who fear Him. They become one with Him; that is, they are identified by Him and take upon His attributes by adhering to His righteous commandments.

In the Old Testament, God revealed that He was the Supreme God. He is the only God to be worshiped and feared. He gave Israel many names so that they could identify Him in some way, though no one name describes His fullness.

Before God could send His Son into the world, He revealed Himself. This was to ensure that when the Son appeared, they would be able to trust Christ's message and ministry because it would reflect the God that was revealed under the Old Covenant.

Therefore, we discover that the Father exists

distinctly from the Son. He, through the prophets, revealed that His Son would come. God gave witness of Himself. When the Son came, He established that witness by performing and doing all that the Father had purposed. In this, we understand that there is only one true God who revealed Himself to man through His Son. The words of Moses still ring true, "Hear O' Israel, the Lord our God is one Lord."

Chapter 4:

Sit Thou at My Right Hand
Psalm 110:1

During His earthly ministry, Jesus faced
constant criticism and opposition from the religious
leaders of the day. The Pharisees and Sadducees
tried to undermine Him through deceitful questions;
hoping to trap Him in His words. However, Jesus
consistently confounded them. The gospels record
that those that heard Him were always "astonished
at His doctrine."

And when the multitude heard this, they
were astonished at his doctrine. Matt 22:33
(KJV)

After one of these instances, Jesus confronted
the Pharisees with their own devices. He asked them

a question. Matthew records,

> While the Pharisees were gathered together, Jesus asked them, Saying, What think ye of Christ? Whose son is he? They say unto him, The Son of David. He saith unto them, How then doth David in spirit call him Lord, saying, The LORD said unto my Lord, Sit thou on my right hand, till I make thine enemies thy footstool? If David then call him Lord, how is he his son? And no man was able to answer him a word, neither durst any man from that day forth ask him any more questions. Matt 22:41-46 (KJV)

Christ's words establish biblical truths concerning the Jewish understanding of the Messiah, David's connection to the Messiah, and the interpersonal dynamics of the relationship between the Father and the Son.

The Jewish people understood that the Christ would be the descendant of David. They understood that He would be a righteous King who would bring restoration and deliverance to God's people. However, they did not fully comprehend the deity of the promised Messiah.

Remember, David was a prophet and king, so they could understand that the Messiah would come as God's messenger in conjunction with His rule. Yet, they missed the spiritual implications of His coming; that is, He would come as the only begotten Son of God.

Though there is much to be explored concerning these truths, we must turn our attention towards the latter parts of Jesus' statements. Amid His challenge, He quotes one of the Psalms,

The LORD said unto my Lord, Sit thou at my right hand, until I make thine enemies thy footstool. Psalms 110:1 (KJV)

This verse not only reveals the deity of Christ, but it also demonstrates to us the interpersonal relationship of the Father and the Son. We see that there are conversations that take place between them. This is a direct contradiction of the belief that God and Jesus Christ are one and the same. Though they are one, they are distinctive in existence. Though Jesus used this verse to establish His deity, we discover it solidifies the eternal existence of the Father and the Son; characterized by heavenly communication.

Some have tried to reconcile this verse with the Oneness doctrine by implying that it is an instance of God speaking to Himself. However, the words are clear that God is not saying to Himself to sit at His own right hand. It does not make sense. In addition, we do have an account of God speaking concerning Himself in His promise to Abraham,

And said, By myself have I sworn, saith the LORD, for because thou hast done this thing, and hast not withheld thy son, thine only son: That in blessing I will bless thee, and in multiplying I will multiply thy seed as the stars of the heaven, and as the sand which is upon the sea shore; and thy seed shall possess the gate of his enemies. Gen 22:16-17 (KJV)

So, we discover that if God spoke to Himself or concerning Himself, it can be understood plainly, not needing any search for interpretation. Furthermore, looking at the construction of Psalm 110:1, in the Hebrew language, dissolves any doubt that God was speaking to and of another; that is, Christ. Let's look at the verse again.

The LORD said unto my Lord, Sit thou at my right hand, until I make thine enemies thy footstool. Psalms 110:1 (KJV)

In the English translations, we see the word Lord used twice (Lord said unto my Lord). However, in the Hebrew two different words are used for Lord. The first 'Lord' in this verse is the Hebrew word Yahweh or Jehovah, the same name God used to reveal Himself to Moses as the Self-Existent or Eternal God.

The second 'Lord' in this verse is the Hebrew word Adonai, which means King or Master. Hence, the verse reads in this sense, "The Eternal God said to the King…"Numerous passages of scriptures attest to the kingship and lordship of Christ. He is repeatedly called king, ruler, lord, and master.

Therefore let all the house of Israel know assuredly, that God hath made that same Jesus, whom ye have crucified, both Lord and Christ. Acts 2:36 (KJV)

Hence, we understand that God was speaking

to the Son whom He made 'king of kings' and 'lord of lords.' In addition to the verse in Psalm 110, other scriptures establish the distinct personalities of the Father, the Son, and the Holy Spirit in interpersonal communication.

The Father Said to the Son

Both Testaments give record of the Father speaking to Jesus Christ. As we examine these, we further establish the uniqueness of the Father and the Son. Many of David's psalms included prophecies concerning the Messiah. As with Psalm 110, other psalms prophetically reveal communication between the Father and the Son. Even the latter part of Psalm 110 reveals more communication of the Father towards the Son.

The LORD hath sworn, and will not repent, Thou art a priest for ever after the order of

Melchizedek. Psalms 110:4 (KJV)

After declaring the kingship of Christ whose enemies will be conquered, David continues by prophetically showing the Father establishing Christ's priesthood. The Father gave an oath concerning the priesthood of Christ. He told Christ that He was a priest after the order of Melchizedek. The writer of Hebrews establishes that this verse is expressly speaking of God talking to Christ.

> So also Christ glorified not himself to be made an high priest; but he that said unto him, Thou art my Son, today have I begotten thee. As he saith also in another place, Thou art a priest for ever after the order of Melchisedec. Heb 5:5-6 (KJV)

Again, the construction of this verse in Psalm 110 portrays God talking to Christ and not of

Christ (demonstrated by God saying, "thou"). When Christ entered the world, therefore He said,

> For I have not spoken of myself; but the Father which sent me, he gave me a commandment, what I should say, and what I should speak. And I know that his commandment is life everlasting: whatsoever I speak therefore, even as the Father said unto me, so I speak. John 12:49-50 (KJV)

Christ testified that everything He said and did, He did at the command of the Father. Though the Son is eternal like the Father, He is always seen in subjection to Him. This explains why we have record of conversations that establish this truth. Hence, Christ refers to Himself as a king and priest because the Father decreed it. He calls Himself the Son of God because the Father called Him, Son.

God hath fulfilled the same unto us their children, in that he hath raised up Jesus again; as it is also written in the second psalm, Thou art my Son, this day have I begotten thee. Acts 13:33 (KJV)

We see Paul quoting Psalm 2 which reveals that the Father said to Jesus that He was God's 'Son.' This along with the aforementioned verses all derived from Old Testament passages. Nevertheless, these verses do not stand alone. In the New Testament, we find that God publicly and not prophetically speaks to and of the Son. This again establishes communication between them, refuting claims that they are the same. Consider the following verses:

At Jesus' Baptism

And lo a voice from heaven, saying, This is my beloved Son, in whom I am well pleased. Matt 3:17 (KJV)

The Father speaks from heaven declaring Jesus as His Son that all may hear.

At His Transfiguration

> While he yet spake, behold, a bright cloud overshadowed them: and behold a voice out of the cloud, which said, This is my beloved Son, in whom I am well pleased; hear ye him. Matt 17:5 (KJV)

God speaks to the disciples at Jesus' transfiguration declaring that He is God's Son.

At Jesus' Entrance into Jerusalem

> Now is my soul troubled; and what shall I say? Father, save me from this hour: but for this cause came I unto this hour. Father,

glorify thy name. Then came there a voice from heaven, saying, I have both glorified it, and will glorify it again. John 12:27-28 (KJV)

Jesus prays to the Father and God responds to Him. Here is direct communication between the Father and the Son while Jesus lived as a man. Some try to purport that when Jesus, as a man, communicated and prayed to the Father, He was speaking to Himself. If this were true, then God would have reduced Himself to parlor tricks and induce confusion in those that came to Him.

Both Testaments are clear that the Father and the Son exist separately though they operate in total unity.

The Son Said to the Father

In addition to the record of the Father speaking to the Son, we have numerous New Testament accounts of Jesus, in his earthly ministry, speaking to the Father. However, the Old Testament gives us a few accounts of Christ speaking to the Father. David, in Psalm 40, gives us an account of Jesus speaking to the Father.

> Then said I, Lo, I come: in the volume of the book it is written of me, I delight to do thy will, O my God: yea, thy law is within my heart. Psalms 40:7-8 (KJV)

Jesus speaks to the Father of the uselessness of sacrifice and burnt offerings and that He would come into the world to do the Father's will. The writer of Hebrews again helps us to understand that this truly is Christ speaking to God.

> Wherefore when he cometh into the world, he saith, Sacrifice and offering thou wouldest

not, but a body hast thou prepared me: In burnt offerings and sacrifices for sin thou hast had no pleasure. Then said I, Lo, I come (in the volume of the book it is written of me,) to do thy will, O God. Heb 10:5-7 (KJV)

The 'he' in this verse is Christ. He says these things unto God. Also, we discover here that Christ says that the Father prepared Him a body. We yet see Christ in subjection to the Father as an obedient Son.

We have stated that there are numerous accounts of the Son speaking to the Father while He walked the earth. But, there is one passage that must be considered in this section.

John 11 gives us the story of Lazarus' resurrection. Jesus' prayer at Lazarus' tomb help us to establish some truths previously discussed as well as demonstrate communication between the Father and the Son.

> Then they took away the stone from the place where the dead was laid. And Jesus lifted up his eyes, and said, Father, I thank thee that thou hast heard me. And I knew that thou hearest me always: but because of the people which stand by I said it, that they may believe that thou hast sent me. John 11:41-42 (KJV)

In His prayer, Jesus establishes that He and the Father communicate. This is demonstrated by the words "thou hearest me always." This denotes continual communication. In addition, at the end of His prayer, He states that He prayed to the Father that the people would believe that the Father sent Him. This again establishes that He and the Father are separate.

Though we have numerous references to communication between the Father and the Son, are there any scriptures that denote communication with the Holy Spirit? We learn from Jesus' words to the disciples that the Holy Spirit would never speak of Himself; whatever He hears that will He speak.

> Howbeit when he, the Spirit of truth, is come, he will guide you into all truth: for he shall not speak of himself; but whatsoever he shall hear, that shall he speak: and he will shew you things to come. He shall glorify me: for he shall receive of mine, and shall shew it unto you. John 16:13-14 (KJV)

From this, we discover that the Holy Spirit is in constant communication with the Father. He can only speak once there has been communication from the Father and Son. Thus, we see continual communication in the heavens.

We can assuredly stand on the biblical truth that the Father, the Son, and the Holy Spirit each exist independently while operating as one. From this chapter, we understand this truth for communication takes place between them. This truth does not support the mythology of polytheism. It again establishes that the Father, the one true God, did all things as it has pleased Him through the Son and the Holy Spirit.

In our next chapter, we will discuss Jesus as the Son of God. Though He is to be worshiped as God (by the Father's command), He abides continually as the Son.

Chapter 5:
Thou art My Son
Psalm 2:7

Though Jesus Christ is worshiped as God, He eternally exists as the Son of God. This is a great mystery. How can God have a Son? As humans, we only understand parenthood in light of a birth. Thus, the advocates of the Oneness doctrine use this limited concept to deny that Jesus is God's Son, eternally. They suppose that God calls Christ "Son" only because of the natural birth through Mary.

In this chapter, we want to bring understanding to the Fatherhood of God and the Sonship of Christ. The scriptures are clear that Christ is the SON of God, not only when He came in the flesh, but eternally. From the scriptures, we can assuredly state that Christ is the Son of God, thus, making Him separate from the Father. In the Law, every word (in terms of legal accusations and affirmations) was to be established by two or three witnesses.

> One witness shall not rise up against a man for any iniquity, or for any sin, in any sin that he sinneth: at the mouth of two witnesses, or at the mouth of three witnesses, shall the matter be established. Deut 19:15 (KJV)

We have multiple biblical witnesses that Christ exists eternally as the Son of God. Again, this establishes His uniqueness in relation to the Father.

The Testimony of Fallen Angels

Let us begin this section by understanding that we are never to formulate doctrine from the devil. However, from scriptural records, we see that the devil and demons know the truth concerning

God and Christ.

The gospels attest that the Holy Spirit led Jesus into the wilderness to be tempted of the devil. After fasting for forty days and nights, the devil appeared to test Him. In his attempts to defeat Christ, the devil opens his first two arguments by challenging the sonship of Christ.

> And when the tempter came to him, he said, If thou be the Son of God, command that these stones be made bread. Matt 4:3 (KJV)

> And saith unto him, If thou be the Son of God, cast thyself down: for it is written, He shall give his angels charge concerning thee: and in their hands they shall bear thee up, lest at any time thou dash thy foot against a stone. Matt 4:6 (KJV)

When the tempter appears, he calls Jesus'

sonship into question. When individuals doubt that He is eternally the son of God, they are walking in the way of the enemy. If Jesus were not God's Son, the adversary would not have used that in his temptation of Christ. But, the record shows that he did; affirming that God sent His Son, not that Jesus became His Son through birth. Not only did the devil recognize Christ as God's Son, but the demonic spirits that encountered Him also.

> And when he was come to the other side into the country of the Gergesenes, there met him two possessed with devils, coming out of the tombs, exceeding fierce, so that no man might pass by that way. And, behold, they cried out, saying, What have we to do with thee, Jesus, thou Son of God? art thou come hither to torment us before the time? Matt 8:28-29 (KJV)

> And unclean spirits, when they saw him, fell

down before him, and cried, saying, Thou art the Son of God. Mark 3:11 (KJV)

In each of the above passages, we discover that the demons called Jesus Christ the SON of God. In the case of the two demoniacs, they recognized Christ as God's Son in relation to eternal events.

They asked was the Son of God coming to torment them before the time. They recognized Christ as the Son of God who would judge all things in the end. This is why James wrote,

Thou believest that there is one God; thou doest well: the devils also believe, and tremble. James 2:19 (KJV)

James establishes the demonic forces' knowledge of the truth of God. He states that they believe that there is one God. We understand this to refer to the

Father. Thus, when the demons encountered Christ, they called Him the Son of God rather than solely GOD.

The Testimony of God and Father

Some may argue that the above references do not substantiate the claim that Jesus is the Son of God. They may still want to assert that Christ was God the Father when He came in the flesh. However, the testimony of God is that Jesus Christ was and is His Son. They are not one and the same.

Again, considering Psalm 2, we discover that before Christ came in the flesh, God declared Him as Son.

> I will declare the decree: the LORD hath said unto me, Thou art my Son; this day have I begotten thee. Psalms 2:7 (KJV)

Some of the Oneness advocates say that this scripture is prophecy; that is, it is predicting Jesus Christ's birth through Mary as the Son of God. However, this is due to a misunderstanding of the word "begotten" and the expression "this day."

We stated at the beginning of this chapter, that humans only understand parenthood and sonship in terms of natural childbirth. Hence, God declaring that He begat Christ seems only possible in light of Mary's delivery of Him. However, this is simply not the case.

The term "begotten" in the Hebrew carries different connotations. Therefore, in Genesis, we find the generations of men recorded by listing fathers who begat children. We know that men (males) do not have children, but their children are their offspring, lineage, heritage, and pedigree.

This is the implication of "begotten" in

Psalm 2. God was declaring Christ's pedigree and lineage, not His manner of birth. In addition, begotten refers to Christ's being. He could only be the begotten of God through possessing the same attributes of God. Unlike the angels who were created, Christ was not a creation of God, but a reflection of Him.

> Being made so much better than the angels, as he hath by inheritance obtained a more excellent name than they. For unto which of the angels said he at any time, Thou art my Son, this day have I begotten thee? And again, I will be to him a Father, and he shall be to me a Son? And again, when he bringeth in the firstbegotten into the world, he saith, And let all the angels of God worship him. Heb 1:4-6 (KJV)

Christ was better than the angels because He was not created, but an eternal extension of God.

The verse says God brought the first begotten into the world. Christ was the only begotten Son of God before His birth by Mary.

In understanding this, when God (in Psalm 2) says "this day," it is a prophetic denotation of time. As long as there is a day, God calls Christ His Son. Since God is eternal, the "day" never ends, so the sense of this verse reads, "You are My Son, eternally have I declared your lineage." God testifies that Christ is the Son for eternity. In the book of Isaiah, it records that God's arm brought salvation to Israel.

And he saw that there was no man, and wondered that there was no intercessor: therefore, his arm brought salvation unto him; and his righteousness, it sustained him. Isaiah 59:16 (KJV)

An arm is an extension of the body. It

represents the body's strength and is made of the same substance of the body. The Oneness supporters say that this shows that God and Christ were one and that God was Israel's salvation personally. Yet, this verse says His arm; that is an extension of Himself.

We know that this is a direct reflection of Christ. He came in the express image of God, reflecting God's strength, power, and personality. Since God is eternal, His arm is eternal; that is, Christ is eternal. He eternally exists as the Son: before His earthly appearance and after His resurrection.

Time would fail to list all the other scriptures of where the Father testifies of Christ as His Son. In chapter 4 (pages 49-54), we discussed conversations between the Father and Son. Listed there are other references to the Father's claim that Jesus was and is His Son. These only substantiate the Old Testament writings.

The Testimony of the Only Begotten

Some dishonest scholars and theologians have tried to assert that Jesus did not claim to be the Son of God. They say that Jesus only claimed to be the Son of Man. A close examination of the gospels reveal otherwise. Jesus affirms that He is the Son of God. The gospel of John confirms this: Jesus heard that they had cast him out; and when he had found him, he said unto him, Dost thou believe on the Son of God? John 9:35 (KJV)

When Jesus heard that, he said, This sickness is not unto death, but for the glory of God, that the Son of God might be glorified thereby. John 11:4 (KJV)

Say ye of him, whom the Father hath sanctified, and sent into the world, Thou blasphemest; because I said, I am the Son of God? If I do not the works of my Father, believe me not. John 10:36-37 (KJV)

Jesus not only referred to Himself as the Son of God, but also continually said that God was His Father in many passages. He clearly portrayed Himself as the Son of God. Even on the night that He was taken into custody Jesus said to the Father,

And now, O Father, glorify thou me with thine own self with the glory which I had with thee before the world was. John 17:5 (KJV)

These words of Christ's prayer establish three truths. First, God is His Father. Second, Jesus possessed the same glory as the Father. Third, Jesus Christ was with God in eternity before all things. Thus, He established Himself eternally as the Son of God.

The Testimony of Christ's Messengers

Jesus' followers also testified that Christ eternally exists as the Son of God. None of their writings promotes the Oneness doctrine; again that, He and the Father are the same. John wrote his gospel and his letters years after Christ's death and resurrection. All his writings clearly affirmed that Christ (though He is to be served as Lord and God) is the Son of God. He wrote:

> But these are written, that ye might believe that Jesus is the Christ, the Son of God; and that believing ye might have life through his name. John 20:31 (KJV)

> These things have I written unto you that believe on the name of the Son of God; that ye may know that ye have eternal life, and that ye may believe on the name of the Son of God. 1 John 5:13 (KJV)

In his writings, John wrote to establish believers in the faith of the Son of God. There is no indication that Christ stop being God's Son after His work in the earth. The writings of all the other apostles also affirm Christ as the eternal Son of God.

In his opening statements in the Book of Romans, Paul establishes Christian thought, practice, and doctrine concerning God, Jesus, and their eternal relationship.

Paul, a servant of Jesus Christ, called to be an apostle, separated unto the gospel of God, (Which he had promised afore by his prophets in the holy scriptures,) Concerning his Son Jesus Christ our Lord, which was made of the seed of David according to the flesh; And declared to be the Son of God with power, according to the spirit of holiness, by the resurrection from the dead. Romans 1:1-4 (KJV)

In these lines, we discover that God has always preached the gospel through the prophets.

We learn that the gospel of God was concerning God's Son. The Holy Spirit's powerful ministry established and declared Jesus to be the Son of God through the resurrection. Again, we see no evidence that Christ and God are one and the same, but that Jesus is God's only begotten Son. Peter's writings also support Christ as the eternal Son of God.

Blessed be the God and Father of our Lord Jesus Christ... 1 Peter 1:3 (KJV)

The tense of these words suggests that presently, God is the Father of Jesus. The writer of Hebrews also supports that Christ eternally exists as God's Son.

God, who at sundry times and in divers manners spake in time past unto the fathers by the prophets, Hath in these last days spoken unto us by his Son…Heb 1:1-2 (KJV)

Again, we see Christ as the Son of God. He was sent as the final revelation of the gospel of God. His life and ministry eternally speak to man for his redemption. Therefore, we assuredly declare that Jesus eternally exists as the Son of God. When one believes on Christ, they believe on the name of the Son of God.

In our next chapter, we will look closely at Jesus' sentiment, "If you have seen me, you have seen the Father." This has been the source of much debate and one of the chief scriptures used by the advocates of the Oneness doctrine.

However, we will prove that it does not suggest that Christ and God are the same, but that

Christ truly came from God and is His Son.

Chapter 6:

Shew Us the Father

John 14:9

Jesus' crucifixion was imminent. He told the disciples of His coming arrest and death. He warned Peter that he would deny Him. He reminds them of the hope of heaven. Jesus reminded them that all who came to the Father had to come by Him. At this point, Philip asks Jesus to show the Father to them. It is here that we find these words,

Jesus saith unto him, Have I been so long time with you, and yet hast thou not known me, Philip? he that hath seen me hath seen the Father; and how sayest thou then, Shew us the Father? John 14:9 (KJV)

This response is one of the pillars of Oneness

thought and doctrine, which seemingly poses a challenge to Trinitarianism. However, the gospels were not written to confuse, but to establish believers in the faith of the Son of God.

We established earlier that God, Christ, and the Holy Spirit were present in the beginning. God created all things by and through Christ. His command to make man in our image and after our likeness was not just rhetoric, but an acknowledgment of Christ who possessed the likeness and image of God.

We also discussed how there were conversations in heaven. Both Testaments reveal interaction between the Father and Son, establishing their individuality. Also, we learned that Christ is eternally the Son of God. Thus, Christ's words to Philip are recorded not to abolish the existence of the Father and Son concurrently, but to establish it. How then should we regard His words?

Without contradiction to the revelation of scriptures, Christ's words simply meant that anything they could learn and know of the Father had been demonstrated in His life. Hence, if you had seen Christ, you (really) had seen the Father.

Some might say, "No sir, you are putting a slant on His words!" However, if one continues to read the verses after this Jesus still refers to the Father as being distinct from Himself.

> Believest thou not that I am in the Father, and the Father in me? the words that I speak unto you I speak not of myself: but the Father that dwelleth in me, he doeth the works. Believe me that I am in the Father, and the Father in me: or else believe me for the very works' sake. John 14:10-11 (KJV)

Jesus says that all that He preached and

performed was because of the Father. When He states that the Father is in Him and He is in the Father, He was not making a theological statement concerning literal oneness, but of how He and the Father are in total agreement.

As Christians, we are said to be the Body of Christ and to be one with Him. However, we retain our individuality though we abide in Him. This is the same principle with Jesus and the Father. Yet, some will still say that this is a matter of interpretation. Well, let us look to the scriptures to establish the presented viewpoint.

The Vision of Daniel

We discovered that the Hebraic use of the term elohim to describe God was not in reference to His plurality, but to His supremacy above anything that is called 'god.' The Hebrews were to worship only one God.

We know in hindsight from the New Testament that the one true God sent His Son who is to be worshiped in honor of God. Though the full revelation of Christ was to come, God still spoke to the prophets of Christ's coming and rule.

The Book of Daniel contains profound visions and prophecies of the end times. Daniel's visions told of Christ's earthly ministry as well as His eternal rule with the Father. It is from this, we discover one of the greatest truths, which gives clear evidence of the intent of Christ's statement, "he that hath seen me, hath seen the Father."

> I beheld till the thrones were cast down, and the Ancient of days did sit, whose garment was white as snow, and the hair of his head like the pure wool: his throne was like the fiery flame, and his wheels as burning fire. Dan 7:9 (KJV)

Daniel's vision foretells the culmination of all things and places God the Father, sitting on the throne. We see two descriptors of His appearance: garment white as snow and hair was like pure wool. Continuing, Daniel reveals that the Ancient of days is giving power, dominion, and authority to another.

> I saw in the night visions, and, behold, one like the Son of man came with the clouds of heaven, and came to the Ancient of days, and they brought him near before him. And there was given him dominion, and glory, and a kingdom, that all people, nations, and languages, should serve him: his dominion is an everlasting dominion, which shall not pass away, and his kingdom that which shall not be destroyed. Dan 7:13-14 (KJV)

Without contradiction, we understand that this is a clear reference to Jesus Christ. He called

Himself the "Son of man" repeatedly. Hence, we discover that Christ is to be worshipped because God gave dominion to Him. Also, we see God and Christ existing distinctly; that is, separately in heaven.

The appearance of Christ on earth was not a modalistic act of God, He was the Son of God coming in the name of His Father. Because of His obedience and submission, all are to worship, honor, and adore Him in obedience and to the glory of the one true God.

And that every tongue should confess that Jesus Christ is Lord, to the glory of God the Father. Phil 2:11 (KJV)

This is the mystery of how Christians are monotheistic. The one true God commands men to honor and worship His Son. When we worship Christ, it brings honor and glory to God.

Before proceeding further, we want to focus on the two descriptors given of God's appearance. Again, He is said to be clothed in a white garment, with hair as white as wool. Now, let us look at John's description of Christ given in Revelation, chapter 1.

And in the midst of the seven candlesticks one like unto the Son of man, clothed with a garment down to the foot, and girt about the paps with a golden girdle. His head and his hairs were white like wool, as white as snow; and his eyes were as a flame of fire. Rev 1:13-14 (KJV)

When comparing these two passages, we discover that Jesus Christ and the Father share identical characteristics with some distinctions placed upon Christ. Each possessed hair as wool and a long white garment. This helps us to grasp further Jesus' statements to Philip.

Even in Christ's appearance to John, He was revealing what the Father was like. This demonstrates again the oneness of God and Christ. Jesus' statement does not establish that He and the Father are one and the same, but it does establish that Christ was with God, came from God, and that He is God's Son. Thus, to behold Him is to behold the Father because He came from Him.

Jesus' Perspective of His Earthly Ministry

The flaw of some biblical interpretation is that it is tainted by an individual's perspective rather than by the biblical narrative. We stated earlier that Christ's words did not come to confuse but establish truth. To understand His words, we must consider Christ's perspective and not our personal opinions. Throughout His ministry, Jesus declared that everything that He did in submission and obedience to the Father. He said that His word and doctrine were from the Father.

For I have not spoken of myself; but the Father which sent me, he gave me a commandment, what I should say, and what I should speak. John 12:49 (KJV)

Jesus attributed the healings, miracles, and many wonderful works to the Father.

But Jesus answered them, My Father worketh hitherto, and I work. Then answered Jesus and said unto them, Verily, verily, I say unto you, The Son can do nothing of himself, but what he seeth the Father do: for what things soever he doeth, these also doeth the Son likewise. John 5:17, 19 (KJV)

Christ makes many similar statements during His ministry. These form the foundation for His statement to Philip. Christ testified that He said and did all things at the Father's command. Whatever He saw the Father doing that is what He did. His life was a demonstration of the Father at work.

Consequently, for Philip to ask Him to show the Father to them was an ill-advised request. They had seen the Father working through Christ the entire time and had not realized it. Therefore, His statement only verifies this truth, not that He and the Father are one and the same.

The Apostles' Understanding of God and Christ

The apostles' teachings on the relationship between Christ and God establish our argument thus far. They taught that (as Jesus said) to behold Christ was to see the Father; that is, His nature, His divinity, and His will. Paul wrote these words,

In whom we have redemption through his blood, even the forgiveness of sins: Who is the image of the invisible God, the firstborn of every creature: Col 1:14-15 (KJV)

Christ came in the image of the invisible
God. What could be learned of God was revealed
in Christ. The writer of Hebrews asserts the same
argument.

> Who being the brightness of his glory, and
> the express image of his person, and
> upholding all things by the word of his
> power, when he had by himself purged our
> sins, sat down on the right hand of the
> Majesty on high. Heb 1:3 (KJV)

Not only is Christ seen as the express image
of God, but He also is seen seated at God's right
hand. If they were one and the same, this statement
would be ridiculous. John establishes our present
affirmations also.

No man hath seen God at any time; the only

begotten Son, which is in the bosom of the Father, he hath declared him. John 1:18 (KJV)

No man has even seen God. In the Old Testament, men would only have visions of the Father where His face and His form could not be fully described because of His brightness. Consider Ezekiel's description.

and upon the likeness of the throne was the likeness as the appearance of a man above upon it... from the appearance of his loins even upward, and from the appearance of his loins even downward... Ezek 1:26-27 (KJV)

In addition, God's words and prophetic counsel were filtered through the prophets and the teachings of the Law, which could add to ambiguity, obscurity, and uncertainty. Thus, Christ came to show the Father to the world, in all His glory, to those who would receive Him. To receive Christ, was and is to receive the Father. This is the underlying context of Christ's statements to Philip.

There was no need of another vision or interpretation of the Law because Christ was not only the Son of God, but also as the Word made flesh. His life and ministry were the perfect reflection of the fullness of God. Jesus conveyed to Philip that God placed all things upon Him and that they did not need to look for anything else.

We are in Union (Matthew 10:30)

This profound statement of Christ is a key thread in the Oneness doctrine and could be a potential flaw in the Trinitarian doctrine. However, this statement was not made to support or refute either doctrine, but to establish the relationship between the Father and the Son. We will look at this from a natural standpoint to verify the truth and meaning of Jesus' words.

> I desired Titus, and with him I sent a brother. Did Titus make a gain of you? walked we not in the same spirit? walked we not in the same steps? 2 Cor 12:18 (KJV)

In his letter to the Corinthians, Paul states that he sent one of his sons in the ministry, Titus. Then, that Titus walked in the same spirit and steps as Paul. Paul was saying that Titus did not say or do anything differently from what he would do.

Now, if one could speak of another human, who is subject to error in this manner, how much the more could this be said of Christ in relation to God? Christ walked as the Father would walk and came in the same Spirit of the Father. There is no division in what God wants and what the Son wants. Therefore, Christ and the Father are one: in spiritual essence and form, and in personality, volition, intent, and will.

Besides, in the verses before and after, Jesus continues to make a distinction between Himself and the Father. Hence, this statement does not speak to the numerical value of Him and the Father, but their union (as the Greek word for "one" in this verse (Mtt. 10:30 illustrates).

Therefore, we understand through biblical insight that if one beheld Christ, He did behold the Father, though they are distinct. Without contradiction and controversy, the Father and Son exist independently, yet succinctly.

Chapter 7:
These Three Give Witness
I John 5:7

Both Testaments are clear concerning the existence of the Father, the Son, and the Holy Spirit distinctively and succinctly. There is no division among them. Again, though these three comprise the fullness of God, it does not substantiate criticism that Christians worship more than one God. We have established that God performed all things through and by the Son. We discovered from the biblical account of Creation, the Holy Spirit was present.

In this chapter, we want to explore the role of the Holy Spirit in God's redemptive work in the earth by Jesus Christ. In his letter, John challenges Christians to walk in the faith of the Son of God.

After reminding them of Christ's divinity and humanity, he speaks of the unity of the Father, the Son, and the Holy Spirit.

> For there are three that bear record in heaven, the Father, the Word, and the Holy Ghost: and these three are one. 1 John 5:7 (KJV)

The Holy Spirit's work is essential to the completion of God's plan and eternal purpose. Understanding His role completes the believer's assurance of God's salvation through Jesus Christ. The Holy Spirit is God's agent in the earth.

He is responsible to reveal God's nature, power, and eternal purpose. He was present at Creation as the tangible presence of God effecting His creative words. Throughout the Old Testament, the Holy Spirit spoke to the prophets and rested upon Israel's priests and kings.

Earlier, we discussed the Holy Spirit's relationship to the Father and Son. Jesus stated that the Holy Spirit would not speak of Himself, but what He hears is what He will say. The Holy Spirit can be honored as God because He will reveal the mind and heart of God perfectly. Detractors of the Trinitarian doctrine find it difficult to understand how the Holy Spirit is God.

The Holy Spirit is God because He is the tangible presence of God revealing the unchanging nature of God. Even in the book of Acts, Peter referred to the Holy Spirit as God. The Holy Spirit is a distinct person because He can be grieved and blasphemed (which Jesus says there is no forgiveness for doing).

We must now turn our attention to the work of the Holy Spirit in God's redemptive work; including His work by Jesus Christ.

The Holy Spirit is the Father's Witness

One of the primary roles of the Holy Spirit is to reveal the presence and nature of the eternal God. Before the worship of God (the Father) was institutionalized and formalized, the Holy Spirit convicted men of their sins from the beginning (though they were unresponsive).

> And the LORD said, My spirit shall not always strive with man, for that he also is flesh: yet his days shall be an hundred and twenty years. Gen 6:3 (KJV)

The Holy Spirit revealed to men the eternal holiness and righteousness of God which they ignored, which resulted in the Flood. Subsequent generations also rejected the knowledge of God, which had been imparted to man through the Spirit.

Because that which may be known of God

is manifest in them; for God hath shewed it unto them. For the invisible things of him from the creation of the world are clearly seen, being understood by the things that are made, even his eternal power and Godhead; so that they are without excuse. Romans 1:19-20 (KJV)

Paul stated that God showed Himself to man. How? Genesis reveals that it was by His Spirit. The Holy Spirit since the beginning has moved upon the earth bringing men into the knowledge of the invisible God. Therefore, all men are held accountable if they reject Him.

The Holy Spirit is the Word's Witness

The Holy Spirit is God's agent of communication and activity in the lives of man. Since God's redemptive work is summed up in Jesus Christ, the Holy Spirit testifies of Christ according to the will of God. Consequently, He is seen alongside God and Christ. He does all things to reveal them completely and perfectly.

The Holy Spirit's presence in the life of Christ is God's testimony of Christ. Jesus said that the Holy Spirit would testify of Him. His tangible presence verifies the work of God in Christ.

This is he that came by water and blood, even Jesus Christ; not by water only, but by water and blood. And it is the Spirit that beareth witness, because the Spirit is truth. 1 John 5:6 (KJV)

The Spirit is truth because He is God's presence. He bears witness that Christ is the Son of God. Jesus spoke of the Spirit's presence in His life while conversing with Nicodemus.

For he whom God hath sent speaketh the

words of God: for God giveth not the Spirit
by measure unto him. John 3:34 (KJV)

The Holy Spirit was sent from God
permanently after Christ's return to the Father to
continually reveal God and Christ. He reveals man's
need for repentance and faith in Jesus Christ.

And when he is come, he will reprove the
world of sin, and of righteousness, and of
judgment: Of sin, because they believe not on
me; Of righteousness, because I go to my
Father, and ye see me no more; Of judgment,
because the prince of this world is judged. I
have yet many things to say unto you, but ye
cannot bear them now. John 16:8-12
(KJV)

The Holy Spirit testifies to the world of its
sin and God's righteous judgment that shall come
upon the face of the earth. He convicts men of sin

bringing them into the knowledge of their need for Christ, God's Son.

The Holy Spirit is an Authoritative Witness

The Holy Spirit reveals God and Jesus Christ not only in men's hearts, but also in demonstrating God's eternal power. Supernatural acts are an authoritative witness of God's existence and willingness to dwell among men in a tangible way.

When God sent Moses to Israel, Moses was given two supernatural signs to show that God was with Him (Exodus 4). We know that this was done through the work of the Holy Spirit. The Holy Spirit confirmed the words of Jehovah to Israel.

Christ's ministry was also accompanied by the Holy Spirit's supernatural activity. Signs and wonders accompanied His presentation of the message of the Kingdom of God. It validated the message of salvation through and by Jesus Christ.

> But if I cast out devils by the Spirit of God, then the kingdom of God is come unto you. Matt 12:28 (KJV)

To correct the erroneous assertions of the Pharisees, Jesus contends that His exorcisms were by the Spirit of God. And if so, the activity was a sure sign of God's kingdom coming to all men.

The Holy Spirit speaks to man's hearts and men's senses to bring them into the knowledge of God and Jesus Christ.

The United Witness

In this chapter, we have discussed how the Holy Spirit is the tangible witness of God's nature, work, and power. He revealed the one true God and

His Son through His supernatural work and ministry. However, His work is to be received as God because it clearly reflects God. The principle scripture for this chapter, again, is found in I John 5:7.

> For there are three that bear record in heaven, the Father, the Word, and the Holy Ghost: and these three are one. 1 John 5:7 (KJV)

John makes this statement to establish that the Father testified of Jesus and so did the Holy Spirit. This statement revealed the unified; that is, united voice of the Trinity. To better understand this, here is the breakdown.

The Father testified of the Son through the Spirit by the Law and the Prophets. This culminated with the Father testifying of Christ during His earthly ministry. The Son testified of the Father and His plan for salvation through the Son. His earthly appearance was to verify the presence of the invisible God. The Son came to testify of the Father's desire for man's eternal salvation.

> And this is life eternal, that they might know thee the only true God, and Jesus Christ, whom thou hast sent. John 17:3 (KJV)

The Holy Spirit testified of Christ as God's Son through His presence and supernatural work in Christ's ministry. Thus, when we read John's words, he is saying that the Father, the Son, and the Holy Ghost speak the same words and establish the same truth of God. These three exist and speak united from heaven revealing the complete council of God.

The Holy Spirit was sent from God to continue the work of Christ through His followers. Since the Holy Spirit is truth and He only speaks of the truth of God in Christ, His works and words are to be received as God's very own. This is at the heart of Trinitarianism.

The Holy Spirit speaks with the same authority of Christ and God because He only speaks what they are speaking. In this sense, He is equal to the Father and the Son. Therefore, we can assuredly state that the Father, the Son, and the Holy Spirit exist separately but never operate in contradiction, disunity, or independently.

Earlier, we established that the Holy Spirit is never said to have God's image or likeness, as does the Son. In the end, the kingdoms of this world will become the "kingdom of our Lord and of His Christ." The Holy Spirit is never said to come into an inheritance as Christ. Therein lies the distinction in the relationship of the Father to the Son and the Holy Spirit.

And out of the throne proceeded lightnings

and thunderings and voices: and there were seven lamps of fire burning before the throne, which are the seven Spirits of God. Rev 4:5 (KJV)

The Holy Spirit is seen around the throne of God (represented by the seven Spirits of God, which speak to the fullness of the Holy Spirit), not seated on God's right hand (like Christ). However, a unified Father, Son, and Holy Spirit are seen together as God's eternal plan and purpose unfolds. These three are one.

Concluding Thoughts on the I John 5:7 Controversy: Some translations of the Bible omit this verse. The chief reason is that it is not see in the oldest available Greek manuscripts. It is claimed that it was a marginal note as a verse. However, two points must be considered as to why the omission is not truly warranted.

First, the absence of it in older manuscripts should not point towards it as an addition, seeing many of the Greek and Latin manuscripts have things missing through simple transmission interruptions, while other manuscripts include them.

Second without this verse, John's argument would not be clear, nor would the Greek grammar upon which it is based would be consistent. In this epistle, John was making a defense against the Gnostics who attributed sin to the natural body of Jesus. Here in chapter 5, he demonstrates that Jesus came by natural means, which was confirmed by the Spirit.

And, in the following verses, He demonstrates that Jesus came from God as a part of the divine nature. Through careful historical documentation, a clear argument can be made for its inclusion as a valid verse. He was arguing Jesus' natural and divine origin: each being attested to by three witnesses.

Numerous books and studied have been published which can clearly defend to the authenticity of this verse as being in the original Greek manuscripts. I invite readers to verify this through further study. One work in particular is *A Vindication of 1 John, v. 7., Objections of M. Griesbach.*

Chapter 8:
Every Knee Shall Bow
Philippian 2:10

Presently, we have established some important spiritual truths. First, it is a fact that there is only one true God. Second, the one true God created the world and did all things through and by His Son who is to be worshiped. Third, the Holy Spirit is God's agent of communication, revelation, and activity.

These three are distinct in existence but unified in all things; which is a clear affirmation of Trinitarian thought and doctrine. Some may still assert that if one worships God and Christ, then that is a form of polytheism. Therefore, the Oneness doctrine seems more applicable to Christianity. In this chapter, we will further substantiate how God and Christ can be worshiped equally yet allow Christianity to remain monotheistic.

God and Christ's Authority

The Bible gives many references to Christ's relationship with God. Both Testaments affirm that Christ's authority, power, and dominion are given to Him.

And without all contradiction the less is blessed of the better. Heb 7:7 (KJV)

No one can receive honor, dominion, and authority except from someone who is greater in authority. This is true of God and Christ. Referring, again, to Daniel's vision of the Son of man, we discover that God gave Christ the authority that He possesses.

I saw in the night visions, and, behold, one

like the Son of man came with the clouds of heaven, and came to the Ancient of days, and they brought him near before him. And there was given him dominion, and glory, and a kingdom, that all people, nations, and languages, should serve him...Dan 7:13-14 (KJV)

This scripture forms the foundation for the worship of God and Christ. From Daniel's vision, we see the Father giving dominion and glory to Jesus Christ. For what cause? It states so that all people, nations, and languages should serve Him.

And that every tongue should confess that Jesus Christ is Lord, to the glory of God the Father. Phil 2:11 (KJV)

The one true God commands all men to

worship Christ. This, again, is why Christians can call themselves monotheists because Christ is worshiped at God's command. We stated earlier, when Christ is worshiped, the Father receives glory. When Christ is served, God receives worship because it pleased Him to commit all things under Christ's authority.

Christ and God's Authority

Jesus continually affirmed that the Father gave His authority to Him. We established earlier that Christ did all things by the Father's command. He came as an obedient Son and Servant in the full authority of the Father. In the principle verse for this chapter, we find Jesus establishing this truth in His prayer to the Father.

Father, the hour is come; glorify thy Son, that thy Son also may glorify thee: As thou has given him power (authority) over all flesh, that he should give eternal life to as many as thou hast given him. And this is life eternal, that they might know thee the only true God, and Jesus Christ, whom thou hast sent. John 17:1-3 (KJV)

God gave Christ power over all flesh. God enabled Christ with the authority to grant eternal life to all that came to Him. This truth brings clarity to other scriptures that seemingly support the Oneness doctrine. However, every place where Christ refers to Himself with the same authority as the Father is understood in light of the truth that God GAVE Christ the authority to do so.

AUTHORITY TO FORGIVE

God invested Christ with His authority and power; including the ability to forgive sins. Jesus confounded the minds of the Pharisees while establishing His authority as God's Son to execute complete judgment.

> Who can forgive sins, but God alone? But when Jesus perceived their thoughts, he answering said unto them, What reason ye in your hearts? Whether is easier, to say, Thy sins be forgiven thee; or to say, Rise up and walk? But that ye may know that the Son of man hath power upon earth to forgive sins… Luke 5:21-24 (KJV)

AUTHORITY IN PRAYER

Christ told the disciples that whatever they asked the Father, in His name, it would be done. After this, He states that anything they asked Christ, it would be done accordingly.

> And whatsoever ye shall ask in my name, that will I do, that the Father may be

glorified in the Son. If ye shall ask any thing in my name, I will do it. John 14:13-14 (KJV)

Christ has the authority to answer prayers. He plainly tells the disciples that anything they asked in His name that HE would do it. Prayers are answered by Him as they are by the Father.

AUTHORITY IN THE KINGDOM OF GOD

God gave complete authority over the kingdom of God to Christ. Therefore, He exercises all dominion in the kingdom; including, judgment. So, when one reads scriptures of men standing before the judgment seat of Christ, it is not to say Christ and God are one and the same, but He has full authority as given to Him by God. Christ substantiates this truth. Consider the following texts:

All things that the Father hath are mine:

Therefore said I, that he shall take of mine, and shall shew it unto you. John 16:15 (KJV)

And all mine are thine, and thine are mine; and I am glorified in them. John 17:10 (KJV)

The authority of Christ is due to the Father's love of Him. Everything that the Father possessed, He committed to Christ. With this, we can understand all of Christ's statements. He did not come as an expression of God, but as God's Son who had authority to do everything that the Father did. He executes judgment, forgives sins, heals, delivers, and saves.

When one understands that everything is given to Christ, His continual presence in God's eternal plans becomes clear. All things were done by and through Christ at the command of God.

The foreshadowing of Christ's coming in the Old Testament reveals His eternal presence and relationship with the Father. We established earlier that Christ is God's Son, reflecting the Father's person, character, nature, form, and being. Consequently, whatever can be said of the Father is said of the Son.

The Names of God and Christ's Authority

This is a point of controversy between Trinitarians and Oneness adherents. Many of the designations and names of Christ are similar to God's. Moreover, in some cases, they are identical. Hence, some assert that this is clear evidence that God and Christ are one and the same.

However, if God invested His authority in Jesus Christ, then Christ cannot be known by any other names than by those that are attributed to the Father.

1. God called Himself the I AM and Christ referred to Himself as I AM.

> And God said unto Moses, I AM THAT I AM: and he said, Thus shalt thou say unto the children of Israel, I AM hath sent me unto you. Ex 3:14 (KJV)

> Jesus said unto them, Verily, verily, I say unto you, Before Abraham was, I am. John 8:58 (KJV)

God revealed Himself to Moses as the self-existent, eternal God. Christ established His eternal presence by claiming this distinction to Himself.

2. God is called the Almighty God and Christ is called the mighty God.

> And when Abram was ninety years old and nine, the LORD appeared to Abram, and said

unto him, I am the Almighty God... Gen 17:1 (KJV)

And his name shall be called Wonderful, Counsellor, The mighty God, The everlasting Father... Isaiah 9:6 (KJV)

God is the Almighty God for He is the source of all and over all, including Christ. Christ is called the mighty God because He came in God's authority. Even in the Book of Revelation when Christ refers to Himself as the Almighty God, it is because He performed all the counsel of God possessing the Father's power and authority.

3. God and Christ refer to themselves as the Alpha and Omega.

And he that sat upon the throne said... I am Alpha and Omega, the beginning and the end. Rev 21:5-6 (KJV)

I am Alpha and Omega, the beginning and the end, the first and the last. Rev 22:13 (KJV)

Both Testaments always portray the Father as "one seated upon the throne." God's use of this designation reveals that He is the beginning and end of all things. Everything finds its beginning and ending in Him. All occurs at His will and volition.

Christ uses this term to denote His eternal existence and to establish the fact that God performed all things by Him. Also, Christ fulfilled God's complete work of redemption and judgment: its implementation and culmination was in Christ.

Many other names are attributed to Christ and God equally. However, names exist which are attributed to Christ only, which denote His distinction from the Father. They also establish His subjection to the Father. Though Christ exercises the authority of the Father, it is not exercised over the Father. Christ is also called a Priest.

The writer of Hebrews says that Christ was **made** a Priest. For Him to be made a priest, it was done at the hands of another.

Whither the forerunner is for us entered, even Jesus, made an high priest for ever after the order of Melchisedec. Heb 6:20 (KJV)

Christ is called an Apostle. Apostles are individuals who are sent. Apostles are sent with the words and message of another governing body. Christ is the Apostle of our faith sent with God's message of redemption.

…consider the Apostle and High Priest of our profession, Christ Jesus. Heb 3:1 (KJV)

Many other unique names are in the

scriptures concerning Christ. However, the above two designations mentioned reaffirm that Christ's authority was given to Him.

We can conclude that God gave Christ authority over all things. Christ executes judgment and volition through His invested authority. This helps men to understand that the worship of Christ establishes the reign and rule of the one true God, who commanded it to be so. This is how God and Christ are worshiped together, yet Christianity remains monotheistic.

Chapter 9:
That God May be All in All
I Corinthians 15:28

Throughout this book, we have explored the different dynamics of the eternal existence of the Father and Son. Scriptural evidence supports their eternal existence and coexistence; refuting the argument that the Father and Christ are one and the same. We also discovered that the Holy Spirit is the tangible witness of God and Christ. He reveals the power and counsel of God perfectly. Thus, He can be honored as God. The Son and the Holy Spirit accomplish the will of the eternal God: these three being one.

To conclude our presentation, we want to make the final distinction between the Father and the Son. We stated earlier that Christ exercises the authority of the Father. However, Christ's authority is not exercised over the Father. When Jesus stated that the Father was greater than Him, He meant it literally. He did not say that just because He was in the form of a man.

> Ye have heard how I said unto you, I go away, and come again unto you. If ye loved me, ye would rejoice, because I said, I go unto the Father: for my Father is greater than I. John 14:28 (KJV)

This statement does not make Christ inferior to God, but it places Him in subjection to God as His Son. Let us regard it in this manner, "God possesses supreme authority while Christ possesses all authority."

This is a great mystery. This reveals that Christ has complete authority over all of creation and the works of God's hands. But, since Christ does not exercise authority over God, this means that God's authority is supreme. As we proceed, this truth will become clear.

The Eternal Purpose Fulfilled

Paul, in his defense of the resurrection to the Corinthians, introduces truths concerning the end of all things, when God's eternal purpose if fulfilled. He begins his discourse by stating that in the end that Christ will deliver the Kingdom up to God, the Father.

> Then cometh the end, when he shall have delivered up the kingdom to God, even the Father; when he shall have put down all rule and all authority and power. For he must reign, till he hath put all enemies under his feet. The last enemy that shall be destroyed is death. For he hath put all things under his feet. 1 Cor 15:24-27a (KJV)

In eternity, Christ remains the Son who came to inaugurate the Kingdom of God. Christ is to reign and rule as King and Lord of all until God's promise to Him is accomplished (making His enemies His footstool). After this, Christ will offer up the kingdom to the Father. This is Christ's final act of submission to the Father.

The Exultation of the Father

God put all things under the feet of Christ. Until the end of all things, Christ remains the central figure (pointing men to the Father) of worship and adoration in God's eternal purposes. However, when the plan of God is accomplished, Christ will become subject to God, in eternity, who placed all things under Christ. 1 Cor 15:27b continues…

But when he saith all things are put under him, it is manifest that he is excepted, which did put all things under him.

Christ's authority does not supersede God's authority. Though God placed all things below Christ, the Father did not place Himself under Christ. In the end, God the Father will be elevated as the central figure of worship for all eternity.

> And when all things shall be subdued unto him, then shall the Son also himself be subject unto him that put all things under him, that God may be all in all. 1 Cor 15:28 (KJV)

These verses establish the eternal relationship of God and Jesus Christ. Christ eternally is the Son who performed all things by the Father's command.

In addition, this establishes that God and Christ are not one and the same or that Christ was God the Father. They exist distinctively orchestrating the affairs of man's salvation.

The Entrance of the Inheritance

Paul's statements may seem challenging to accepted Christian thought. However, they do not contradict it. Though Christ is seen in subjection to God, His offering up the kingdom does not negate His eternal rule and reign. It does however bring clarity to the entrance of Christians into their eternal inheritance with Christ.

The kingdom is referred to the "Kingdom of God and of His Christ." Jesus revealed that He is seated in the throne of His Father. This speaks specifically to His authority to reign and rule over God's creation. Christ's reign does not end with the offering up of the kingdom, it only establishes the supremacy of God's rule in the kingdom (This statement is not in support of subordination theology).

Throughout the writings of the apostles,

Christians are said to be co-laborers and inheritors of the kingdom with Christ. Christ is also called the firstborn among many brothers.

> For whom he did foreknow, he also did predestinate to be conformed to the image of his Son, that he might be the firstborn among many brethren. Romans 8:29 (KJV)

This denotes His eternal relationship and connection with Christians. In eternity, Christians are seen with Christ as having authority, dominion, and rule.

> And if children, then heirs; heirs of God, and joint-heirs with Christ; if so be that we suffer with him, that we may be also glorified together. Romans 8:17 (KJV)

Christ, like the first Adam, will cleave to His bride (the Church) in eternity.

For this cause shall a man leave his father and mother, and shall be joined unto his wife, and they two shall be one flesh. This is a great mystery: but I speak concerning Christ and the church. Eph 5:31-32 (KJV)

Therefore, He offers up the kingdom to God; not only to declare the Father's supremacy, but also to reveal the Christians' entrance as co-inheritors of the kingdom.

And the city had no need of the sun, neither of the moon, to shine in it: for the glory of God did lighten it, and the Lamb is the light thereof. Rev 21:23 (KJV)

Christ will dwell among the people as Lord, Savior, and Friend in eternity. He will be their light for all time. Therefore, let us assuredly declare that the Father and the Son exist distinctively, yet succinctly.

The Son did all things by the Father's command; the Holy Spirit bearing witness to all these things. The coming of Christ brought about the entrance of the kingdom of God and a complete revelation of the Father.

> And the Word was made flesh, and dwelt among us, (and we beheld his glory, the glory as of the only begotten of the Father,) full of grace and truth. John 1:14 (KJV)

He did not come to replace the Father, but as the Son of God coming to reveal His Father to a world that had rejected Him. In understanding these things, we can understand the greatest mystery of God, revealing Himself in Christ.

www.ingramcontent.com/pod-product-compliance
Lightning Source LLC
Chambersburg PA
CBHW020514100426
42813CB00030B/3238/J